I'm Getting New Glasses!

Beth Ann Ramos

good day
BOOKS

For:

_____

You look great in your new glasses!

Written and Illustrated by Beth Ann Ramos
Published by Good Day Books
First Edition

Learn more at www.bethannramos.com.

good day
BOOKS

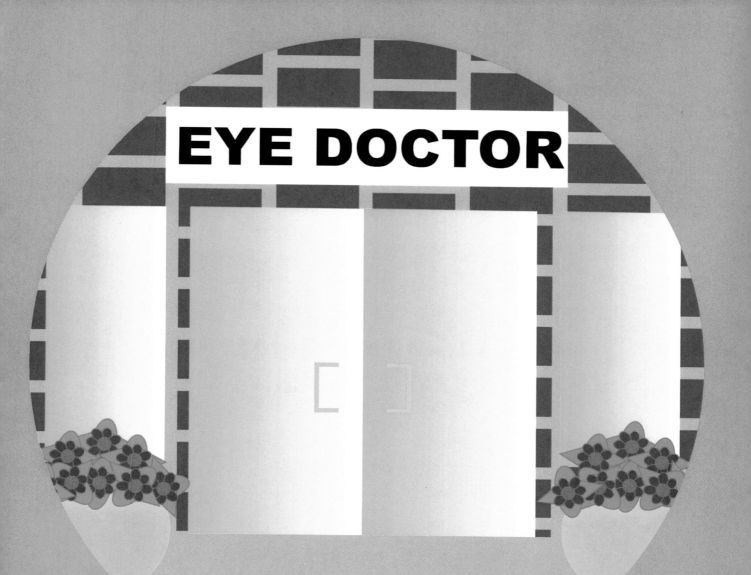

I'm getting new glasses!
Today is the day!

I'll get to see clearly
at school and at play.

I can choose from so many!
Which one is just right?

I can't help but wonder.
Which ones will I like?

Do these make me look silly?

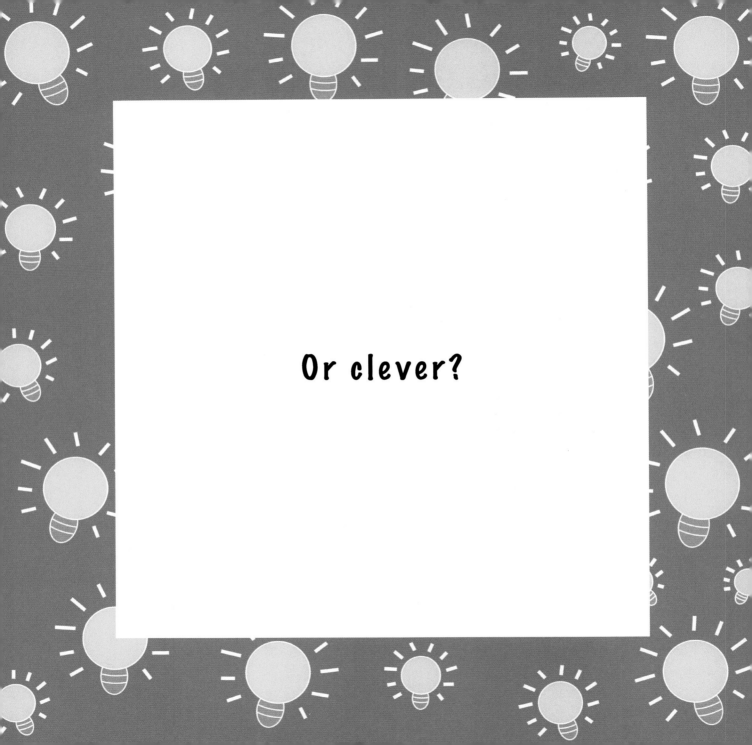

Or clever?

But these match my feet!

These make me feel fancy!

Or sweet?

This pair is cool!

This pair looks retro.

These make me want to play
out in the pool.

Oh look! Now I've found them!
The best pair of all!

Not too big or too little,
or shiny or small.

This pair is my favorite!
They'll help me to see!

They're one of a kind
and as special as me!

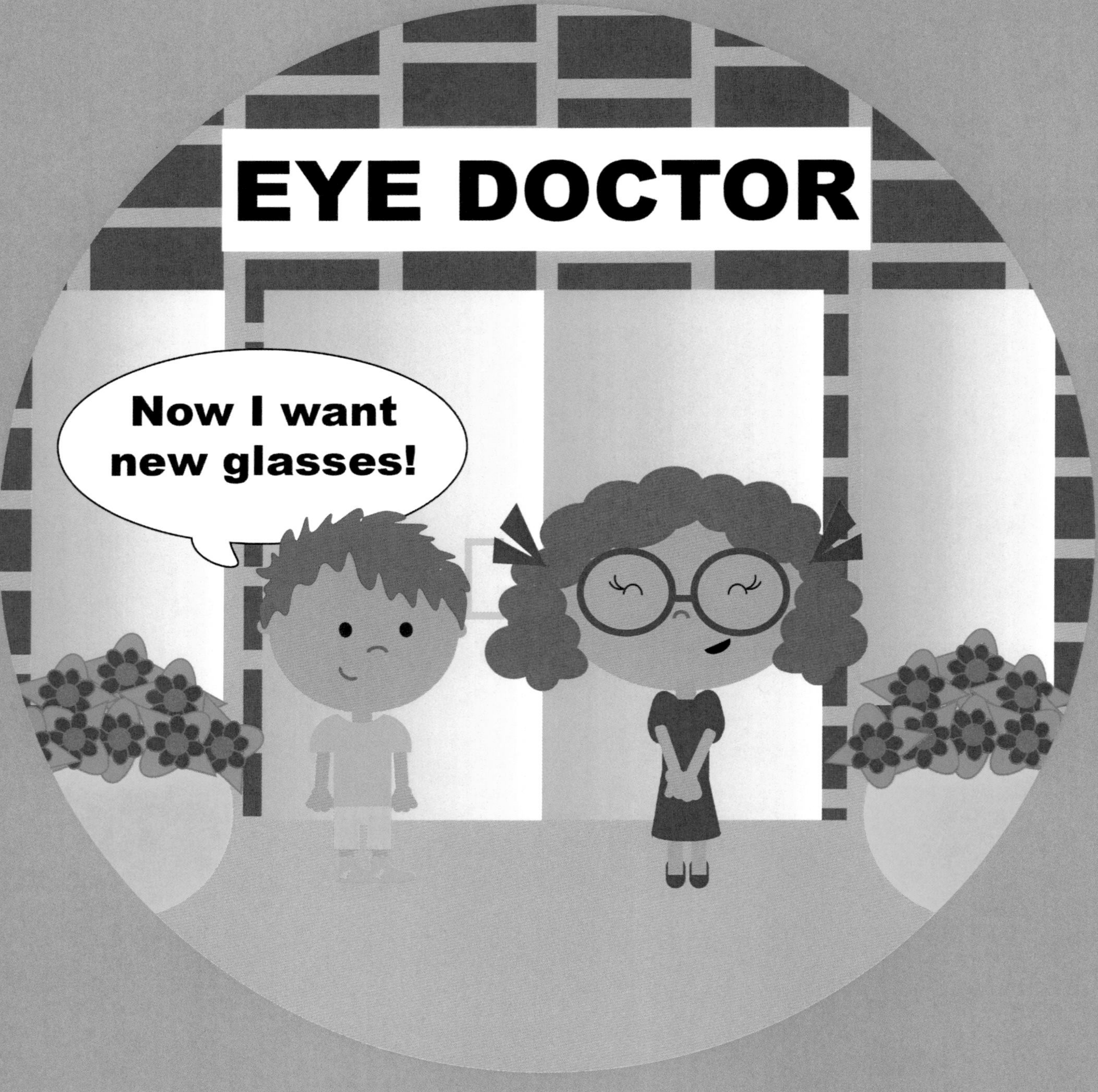
EYE DOCTOR
Now I want new glasses!